MISFORTUNES

OF THE

MISUNDERSTOOD

Q'shaa Myiaa Pollock

Acknowledgments

I keep going back and forth with this page because this book goes out to way too many people.

Grandma, when I told you I was going to give up writing you literally looked me in my eyes and said "I will fucking kill you" those were your exact words. From that moment on I knew I had to publish at least one book.

Mom, you gave me the wisdom I needed to be a writer and the patience. You always believe in me and my crazy career endeavors. I am forever grateful for a mother like you.

My Father, when I first decided I wanted to write, you were one of the first people I told. You agreed that was a good idea. You later told me my writing was good and to never give up. I now know you listen; you heard me and support me.

Zay, you should be the first person I thank. For always supporting me regardless of our rollercoaster relationship. Also, for my bomb ass cover. Thank you, I am forever grateful for your endless support.

G'anna and Shay, my two broke besties, for being the one to encourage me to "be rich". I'll take my last dying breath for you.

Day, you gave me the ambition, the courage and motivation to get started. You believed in me from day one. You support all my career ventures. I couldn't ask for a better friend.

Last but not least, to my exes! The pain y'all caused is about to pay off!

Preface: The Misunderstood

I've been going through life feeling like I am unheard. Like nobody can hear me. We all have a gift, although you may feel like you don't, your voice is a gift. Your thoughts are a gift. I've decided to share my experience with the world. I've always said, "If I can help ONE person then I did my job". Many people will read this and become confused. I've become the product of my pain. Ultimately, becoming the person who hurt me. I wouldn't say heartless, but I can definitely say I've become careless. Everything has become about me and how I can benefit from it. How is it that someone who was once so broken, becomes the one breaking everything in their path? Because remember not everything that glitters is gold. I have flawed and I am flawed.

I watched my mom hurt to the core. I watched my sister's tear themselves apart. I watched "the love of my life" love someone else. I watched my mind turn on me and make me hate myself. I watched my father (who despite everything I love with my whole heart) walk out. I watched my brother come home after being racial profiled because he "fit the description". I watched my sisters and cousins become the best mothers they can be.

I watched and continue to watch my friends and generations after generations DEFY the odds.

Misfortunes of the Misunderstood is meant to address my struggles, in love, in my head, in life. But it's a way to cope. Writing saved me. I hope reading, navigating, and interpreting my pain helps you cope. Whatever you go through, as alone as you might feel, you aren't alone.

Myiaa's Interlude:

I had to find a way to turn my pain around. I had to learn to see the beauty in people, in situations, and in life again. I had to learn to manifest the greatness I can become if I just apply myself. I had to experience growth, but first I had to hit rock bottom and experience pain. It's sad but true. Nobody's life is always uphill. Eventually, things get rocky, sometimes things get so bad that it literally cannot get worse. But you have to remember that there is always a way back up. As tough as it looks when you're at rock bottom, it's not impossible.

I'm trying to figure out how to be the most open and honest with my readers while keeping the privacy of the people around me. Over the past 10 years or so, I have been through many rough patches. It shows throughout my poetry that there were periods of times where I was not okay. Putting my feelings into writing is probably the most upfront I can be with someone. I'm not good at verbally explaining my feelings, but when my pen hits the paper that's when you know it's real. The love is real, the pain is real.

I learned to turn my hurt into words and make magic. So, I've made magic. Welcome to my magic!

My Neighborhood

My neighborhood?
It's pretty normal.
We don't go all formal
and these boys have crazy hormones

I live in a place where the streets want you to come play
but who knows who gonna be next?
To leave from the hood with no return
I think we all earned some respect

So, let's say Rest In Peace to that lady.
Her boyfriend went all crazy
stabbed her in front of her babies.
What about the fact she died in front of the church?
God, I pray that man hurts

Let's talk about the hustlers.
The ones that got busted though.
I know a lot of them personally
and they don't mean any harm
But daddies somewhere not found
Momma can't hold her own grounds
So, guess who's man of the house now?

What about guns?
That they use to protect themselves.
Every time they pull a trigger
there goes another life.
They don't use any knives,
So, I figure
Every time they release the trigger
The guns say "25 to life".

My neighborhood it sometimes sucks you in
The streets really talk
They try to make you break
Want you to come and play
Doesn't want you to go
And this is what I call home

Message:

My people have been oppressed for so long. We have been profiled because of our skin color. I will never forget the night my brother came home from school and was stopped on our stoop. Apparently, he "looked the part". We later found out that they were looking for my white-skinned neighbor. Imagine the fury in my mother's eyes when she walked into the hallway and saw her ONLY son being detained.

As a kid then, I didn't really understand. But then I heard about Eric Garner, Michael Brown, Sandra Bland, Tamir Rice, Mya Hall and today on March 25th, 2020 it's George Floyd. That's just to name a few. When are we going to say enough is enough? How are we going to say enough is enough? We can't protest because they will "fear for their lives" and what's supposed to be peaceful now becomes a riot.

BLACK LIVES MATTER doesn't mean no lives matter. Black lives matter is a movement for equality. For Black lives to be equivalent to the average white man.

Black in America

We all know I LOVE MY BLACK MEN! So someday I will birth multiracial babies. When do I tell my kid that we live in a world where the system that is supposed to protest and serve us is probably going to be the ones that kill us? Will I have to walk my kid to school every single day, pick them up, take them to after school And as they grow work. Just to make sure that my kid doesn't get discriminated against or doesn't die alone. What if my kid grows up and wants to be a cop? And as a mother, I have to encourage them, And pray they can be the change our community needs, all while thinking there's a high chance my kid will be killed by a cop's hands?

How do I tell my son to love yourself, when half of the world doesn't (because half of the world wouldn't)?

How do I tell my daughter that she should admire her beauty when half of the world wouldn't (because half of the world doesn't)?

How do I teach my kids to live in a society that degrades them, but let them know they are destined for greatness, although the system is designed for you not to be?

Why do I have to question these things when I should have to worry about teaching my son how to be a man and my daughter how to be a woman? Now I have to teach my kids how to be black in America.

Dear Old Me,

Everything will come together, eventually.
And although at the moment it might feel a little hard;
Trust me it will get harder,
But you will prevail.

I wish someone would've told me so much I know now.
Like...
That guy, he doesn't love you. He lusts you.
Because someone who loves you wouldn't disgust you.
Or like the guy that's really going to break your heart,
Is the guy that created it in the first place.
Or that home isn't a place,
It's a person.

You'll learn all of these things.
You'll learn that sometimes you have to meet sucky parts
of life to laugh again.
You'll learn that pain is inevitable
But as much as you can't avoid it
You can and you will survive it.
And those thoughts, they're just thoughts,
You don't wanna hurt yourself, you don't wanna die,
And life will soon become precious
the moment you open your eyes.

Baby girl, better days are coming.
And although right now in my head I'm in hell
In my heart, I'm at peace.
Because your heart was pure, and you loved hard.
And for someone who's experienced so much pain
that's the best part of you.

Your confidence is a little low.
And you pick apart your body in disgust.
But believe me when I tell you
your confidence will rise
you'll love your caramel skin
and thick thighs.

I promise you this
everything will come together.
And I know you're going through it.
Puberty and all this heartbroken bull shit.
You will boss up
and become a "badass bitch".
Because of you
I am who I am.
So, thank you Old Me,
For bringing me to where I stand.

Superwoman

I'm starting to realize I can't save everyone.
And as much as I wanna be superwoman
I can't change anyone.
When things get rough I can't blame anyone
especially not myself
Especially not me.
Because I can't save everyone.
I've tried and I've tried.
I done cried and put up a fight.
But sometimes
the one person I need to save
the only person I should save
Is myself.
I can't be superwoman for anyone
I can't be superwoman for everyone
if I'm not a superwoman for me first.

Underwater

Sometimes I feel like I'm clogged.
Like I'm submerged underwater.
All open holes being filled
my hearing is muffled
everything goes blank.
I feel like I'm choking
gasping for air
trying to get to my feet.
Life feels faint.

I'm trying to paint a picture
of what anxiety feels like.
But word can't describe the sleepless night.
The indecisiveness at a restaurant.
The wanting to hang out
but not wanting to get out of bed.
I've been sleeping all night and day
but I'm still tired by noon.

I try to tune
out all of the word
and remain in a bubble.
Because anxiety makes me feel
Like I'm submerged underwater.

Waiting

This is something unexplainable
something that isn't tamable.
Nobody wants to experience this
yet the best of us do.

Crying without reason.
It's like demons taking over inside
making you feel pain
hurting you in any and every way

This thing
it makes you doubtful and insecure
torturing you daily
and there's no permanent cure

Finally, you'll realize
"I'll never be normal.
No, I'll never be okay.
Because this depression shit kills
I'm just waiting on my day".

Message--

Mental health is just as important as your physical health. Internally in your head, you have to make sure that you're okay because then nothing else matters. It sucks to feel like your own mind is turning against you. But you have to rise up.

The first step is admitting that you aren't okay. Something is wrong, and that's okay. It's hard, trust me if anyone knows it's me. But you will shortly realize, it's okay and you can manage your mental health and live the life you want and deserve.

You cannot live life not admitting that you aren't okay and neglecting the self-care you need to give yourself.

Give yourself TLC before you give that man any!

Another Statistic

One in five
Women will get raped in their lifetime.
Probably by some guy commenting on her light eyes.
"Hey beautiful, where you're heading."
Naturally, she makes a detour to avoid him.
Knowing her location. Circle around the block.
Don't worry I'll be safe.
"No sweetie, please go straight home," God Says.
But she can't hear him
and she fears them.
She soon becomes another statistic.

Two in Ten
they're probably saying it's her fault
in the summer her shorts are too short
in the winter her jeans are too tight.
Why can't she be free to wear what she wants
without being afraid, that they'll blame her
for something he did.

Three in fifteen
this doesn't make it any better.
She'll cover-up in a sweater.
She'll try everything to make herself laugh

To feel safe again.

She'll stay home more, avoiding her mom.

But that won't help

Because rape doesn't only happen outside.

Sometimes it happens in your own house.

Anti-Love Poem

Love,
What are you really here for?
To hurt me?
Make me Happy?
Or all of the above.

It's been a rough time, with you
I went through a lot of tissues
and I finally don't believe in you.

So, there's the door.
We will have no more
No more tears and wanting to die.
This time, I'm letting you fly.

Eight

For eight years
EIGHT YEARS
I was molding a man into the perfect person.
Creating him into this magical man
Not knowing he wouldn't be
My knight and shining armor.

I was creating a man
making the better version of myself
not knowing I wasn't going to receive half of it.
Not even a quarter of what it's worth.

How can you take me
it's like taking a momma from her child.
How could you make me
feel these things I should've never felt
deal with cards I should've never been dealt.

For eight years
I caught myself believing everything I didn't see or hear.
I caught you cheating
foolishly I convinced myself it was a slip-up
you were trying to figure out the new you
the you that I built.

Times a thousand
because it didn't happen just once or twice.

Foolish of me to think I can build a better you.
My biggest fear in a relationship
was to build a man
make him better
for the next woman.

So don't ask me why I'm single
because this is my response.
I'm building a better me
one that would make you want to be a better you
just so you can get me.

Seesaw

This love is like a seesaw
it could never stay balanced.
We were high school sweethearts
"together forever".
Usually, we were equal
but more than often not.

You were always at the top.
Dominate and proud.
Me?
I often found myself at the bottom.
I knew I was better than that
I knew with one jump
I could make it to the top.

But we were like
kids in the playground.
You were the sugar that kept me up.
Our love was a seesaw
one that weighed me down.
I was always on the bottom
putting you up top.
Because all I wanted was your love,
All I wanted was your touch.

We were high school sweethearts
"together forever".
We were lovers and friends
the friendlier the better.
We were kids in the playground.
You were the sugar that gave me a high.
And our love was the seesaw
you liked the way I looked at the bottom
and the only way you would stay is
If I left, you on top.

Nothing Lasts Forever

I misunderstood the "I love you's".
I guess I was such a fool.

They say set it free
if it comes back it's yours.
I don't believe in sayings anymore.
Because if someone loves you
why would they leave you at all?

I kind of misunderstood
the feeling that came with being next to you
making me feel so irreplaceable.

The heart rushing and slurred words.
The I love you's that I always said first.
Believe me
your karma would come.

I misunderstood the plans of our future.
The pain mentally and physically wasn't a part of the
plan.

I guess our relationship was misunderstood
Because your parents thought we would last forever.

But everything comes to an end someday

I guess our day was today.

He started to believe in me.
Now the one I wanted is needing me.
-Karma

Karma

You did some fucked up shit.
But I forgave you.
I hope when my secrets come out
you can forgive me too.
Let me enlighten you
I would've never done what I did
had you not fucked me over.

So, tell me
How prideful can you be?
Because you swear
I mean so much to you
but I think it's because I've taken you back
time after time
girl after girl
lie after lie.
Just for you to say
"You were never really mine".

Or is that why you fucked with me so heavy?
Because I played the pendeja
and let you take me in the back of your Chevy.
Man, you might've fucked me good
but Karma's gonna fuck you even better.

Healing: Admitting/Acknowledging

I had to figure out how to grow from the pain.
Admitting that maybe I am the problem
the root of your game.
Taking a look in the mirror to acknowledge
this is a storm.
And as much as I'm afraid of lightning
the phase will past
the sun will come.

You have to admit the problem to heal.

To heal you have to hurt.

To hurt you have to feel.

To feel you have to love.

Open apology

To the guy who always loved me
the one I could never love back.
The one that I chose to cherish a friendship
because I sort of wasn't ready for all that.

To the guy that would buy me roses
even If I didn't ask.
The guy that called me every night
to make sure I'm straight.
I know I should've loved you.
I know momma wanted me to.
Poppa would've been contempt.
So, I'm sorry that I didn't.

I couldn't fix my heart to love you.
I couldn't fix my mind to make you mine.
Because deep down this was too good to be true
you're too good of a guy.
I didn't wanna hurt you how I've been hurt.
I didn't wanna make feel how I've felt.
Because I couldn't love you how you deserved.

This is an apology
to the one who would never understand.

I'm pretty sure breaking my heart

was never a part of your plan.

But I couldn't fix my heart in the time you wanted

I need to experience life myself

love me

want me.

I just want to say sorry.

I want you to know

I tried not to break your heart.

Although I probably did.

I knew I couldn't love you the way you deserved.

I hope you'll understand someday.

To the guy who always loved me

no matter what.

Lie

Man, you really hurt me.
And I know you were being honest
blatantly honest
transparently honest.
But man, why couldn't you lie to me.

Why couldn't you tell me you want me
put no one else above me.
Tell me that you love everything about me.
Even if it's just a lie.

Because logically
everything you're saying doesn't make any sense to me.
You care but you don't want me.
You love me but can't be with me.
Seems like
everything you're saying is followed with the truth
the blatant truth
the raw truth.
Well the truth hurts
so why couldn't you just lie.

Heal my heart from this pain.
Because

time after time

L after L.

Man, I just need some healing

even if it's just a lie.

Forget the blatant truth

just comfort me.

Just fabricate a story

and tell me you love.

Just heal this pain

and for once

for once make me feel wanted.

Even if it's just a lie.

To the guy, I'm madly in love with.

To the guy I'm madly in love with.
You don't know who you are.
And I'm trying to figure you out.
Because before I tell you I need to know for sure.
I don't want to settle for you
and pretend to be happy.
Because that would hurt more than this does.
That would suck
me breaking my own heart.

We started off as a fling
something I wasn't used to.
But now I'm sort of lost for words
every time that I'm with you.
Which is a shame
because things changed.
This man you are isn't the same.

I'm kind of hoping you'll become the man you were
before.
The one that initially made me wanna risk it all.
I want you to surprise me as you did.
Actually, do something to make me wanna take my
panties off.

I refuse to keep being some late-night booty call.
I don't even know what your face looks like in the
sunlight anymore.

To the guy, I'm madly in love with
I'm kind of waiting for you to love me back.
Constantly telling you
"You'll lose me
if you don't choose me."
Leave and then come back.

I should've fallen out of love with you
when you became who you said you wouldn't.
Started doing things you knew you shouldn't.
But love comes quick, unplanned, and unexplainable.
I'm just waiting for you
to become the man, I know you can.
I guess I gotta see you through.
Wait, until I become
The girl you're "madly in love" with.

He Loves Me ... Not

You're like a flower
I am picking at you to see if you love me.
"He loves me".
"He loves me not".
Started thinking it was me
I wasn't capable of being loved.
Doubt that I would ever find love.

Shortly I realized
you were the one incapable.
Incapable of loving me.
Incapable of being who you portray yourself to be.

But still
I picked at you like a flower.
Solely to see if you love me.
"He loves me".
"He loves me not".
Started realizing it was time to give up
because this wasn't my fault.
Truly and honestly you weren't worthy.

It wasn't me.
It was you.

Because

I was capable.

I am capable.

And what's an L to a diamond

I can't lose.

I'm supposed to be loved.

Beauty and Brains baby

it doesn't get any better.

So, what if he doesn't love me.

It doesn't matter if he loves me.

Because who loves me now is all that matters

and that's me .

I love me.

To Him

This is a message to the guy I fell in love with.
The guy I wasn't supposed to fall in love with
because I knew you had a situation.
Situation with someone else.
A situation I couldn't compare to.
A situation that prevented me
from being with you.
But not enough of a situation
to prevent me from feeling for you
dealing with you
craving you in so many ways.

Looking past all the hurt
looking past all the lies
man, I fell in love with a guy
that wasn't even mine.
If he treats her this way
I know with me it will be no different.
But every night I went to sleep
hoping God would make you wake up different.

This guy
he became my sanity
in a life so insane.

He became my escape
in a world full of pain.

Soon enough the switch flipped .
He became the insanity
fucking with my sanity
fucking with my life.
He became the pain
because I fell in love with him
believe me, he did love me
Just in vain.

Now my minds fucked up
and my heart kinda hurts.
Why can't my mind, heart, and soul
understand no strings attached.
This means no attachment
no attraction.
Just a couple nights together
just a 3 a.m. fuck.
My heart didn't quite understand
This was just a couple empty offerings.
My heart didn't understand
I will be the one to end up without wedding plans.

Naive

Your fingers are in a little too deep
for someone who plans on wearing a wedding ring
from someone who is not me.
And my heart is in a little too deep
for someone who knows
it would never be me.

You see
I thought the best of you
I never wanted less for you.
I saw past your flaws
and ignored all your lies.
It's like a flower that cannot bloom
but it also cannot die.
I love you.
You love me not.

Baby, I tried
To use my hands to cover up the sky.
I clearly don't have 20/20 vision
but I
can clearly see where you were heading with things.
Yet and still
I closed my eyes.

Cause Seeing is deceiving.
and every word you said
I started believing.

You came to me seeking happiness.
But just like Romeo and Juliet
this tragedy drastically took a turn for the worst.
You see I had no clue about her.
And now you're posting her all on Snapchat
talk about a snapback.
Oh shit
Snap crap!

How are you gonna explain this to her?
How you gonna tell her you approached me first?
And how you gonna tell her
that you wanted to meet another
so, you asked for my number?
How you gonna tell
your index finger was a little too deep
in places, it shouldn't be
because her sex game a little too weak?

I just wanna understand
how a man can come down from being with his shawty
and cum down into another...

Yeah, you get the story.

I wanna understand

how a man can play these games?

Claiming all women need to be tamed.

I'm just tryna figure out

who raised these fucking lames?

His Happiness

I just wanted you to be happy
even if that meant I wasn't.
If you being happy
meant I cried myself to sleep.
Man, I was willing
to let my heart to take an L that night
just so you can sleep peacefully.

I truly wanted you to be happy
even if that means I wouldn't be.
So, If I had to put my life on the line
put my happiness aside
man, I swear for you I would've done it.

I was loyal to you
in ways that I shouldn't have been.
Man, I've done things
that I should've never did.
But it was all to keep you safe
keep you happy
keep you amazed.

I was ready to change my whole life for you.
And by life I don't mean moving across town

I mean
my lifestyle
my morals.
I was willing to turn the other cheek
for things I would've never.

I let you take me low.
I let you take
my sanity
my mind.
I'm not sure who drove who crazy
but I know
I would've given it all for you baby.

Man, I was so blinded.
I can't count how many nights
I lost for you.
I swear my happiness was seeing you happy
my heart broke for you.
I took that L
just to see you smile.
I just wanted to keep you happy
while I struggled to smile.

Time

You give things for the person you love.
Eventually, you'll find yourself losing sleep just to talk.
You'll find yourself distracted at an event
because man you miss him.
You'll stare at your phone thousand times
just to see if he messaged you.

But on the other side.
On the other side of that phone
he isn't caring
he's living his life.
Boy is he so happy.
He's hanging with friends
focused on a career, education.
Most importantly himself.

So, don't lose sleep.
Don't stop your life.
Because if he wanted you to coexist in his
he'll make time

Momma always told me
"if there's a wheel there's a way".
But I guess there's no wheels

Because you couldn't find no way
Around "I'm busy today".

You did say you was riding to the wheels fall off.
Well maybe they're gone.
Because your attitudes been a little off.
You've been distant
I'm wondering if there's something that I'm missing.
Maybe we're just growing distant
to avoid
the instant pain that will grow
when we both choose to go.

Life of Misunderstood

This the life of the misunderstood.
The "side chick" who's been lied to too.
He told me ya was through.
He said shit was rocky and you knew.
Knew he was moving on to something better.
Not to be cocky but better is here with me
not you.

When I found out about you
Shit I was already in way too deep.
Time and time again I asked about you
secretly guessing my conscious knew.
Man, I don't know who's the bigger fool
him, me or you.

I promise
my heart goes out to you.
It was never my intentions to hurt another woman
so, my hat comes off to you.
Cause man, we spent a lot of time
we did a lot of things.
I'm trying to wonder
where between seeing me and working
did he have time for other things.

Or is everything he said true.

Man, I didn't wanna play
the "Side Chick" "Side Bitch".
I never wanted to be second.
I never wanted to break up a "Happy Home".
But the home couldn't be that happy
if ya man found me.

3A.M - 3 P.M

I no longer wanna be your 3 A.M.

I kinda wanna be your 3 P.M.

Your "I'm coming home to you baby".

Your "get ready we going out love".

I don't wanna just be your fondle

your fuck.

Your "because my girlfriend acting up".

I wanna be your

rollover good night kiss.

I wanna be what your

in work every night missing.

Your "sweetheart I'll be home soon".

Because my love

I swear I didn't plan this.

I swear I don't know how this happened.

And baby boy I don't wanna leave you speechless.

But I'm falling for you.

You are kind of everything that's been on my wish list.

Never Settle

Woman, we have to stand up for what we deserve. We tend to settle for less because of "love". Love yourself enough to make sure you never settle. Love is something uncontrollable. As much as we think we control it, we don't. Love yourself enough to walk away when they don't love you the way you deserve.

I love you but I love me more.

Eleven: Eleven

Every time I think about what you've done
I get sick to my stomach
I get lost for words
I get heartbroken all over again.
I'm allowing a man to "put me first"
all while knowing I'm second.
I'm allowing a man to break my heart
simply because I'm selfless.

You see this wasn't my intentions.
I swear I didn't wanna fall.
I know these weren't your intentions.
I know you didn't wanna break my heart.
But I did
you did
and together we didn't.

We didn't
fight to see what could've been.
We didn't
leave because it was wrong.
And we didn't
Love.

You didn't
love me nor her.
And I didn't
love me first.
We couldn't see
things clearly.
I mean all up in my head
I had this vision.
It'll be me and you
just chilling.
You would be my new thing
something like my boo thang.
You would be the love I never knew existed.

Now you're just the one I'll always be missing.
You're a distant memory
You're an 11:11 wish
You're the one I always wanted
But the one I never got.

Tell Me

I wanna know why you're with her.
I wanna know not what you see in her
but what you feel with her.
What you feel inside
because baby we can't hide this any longer.
I think our cover's blown.
You're clearly not happy with her
you wouldn't be here with me
if you loved her.
You wouldn't be
feeling me
kissing me
dealing with me.

How happy can you be?
Cause in my eyes, it seems like your only happiness
It comes when you're sitting with me.
Side by side
in the car.
I can't help but notice
that smile I get.
It's much better than your smile with her.

R.O.D

I was trying to be a ride or die
to someone who wasn't even mine.
I was trying to show better things
to someone who really didn't make time.

I mean I get it
people get busy
and we're grown
so sometimes things just "come up".
The question is
how many time are things going to just come up
before you decide to show up
before you decide to choose me?

It's the little things that count.
The small things I'll appreciate.
I'd rather five minutes a day
just to see your face
then no time at all.
I'd rather a FaceTime call
on your way to work
then no response at all.

I found myself stopping my life

putting everything on hold
just because you were outside.
I found myself stalking my phone
just to see if I receive a call
or at least a text at all.

I was trying to be a ride or die
to someone who wasn't even really mine.
But sometimes people don't see how hard you ride
until you park the car.
So, I pulled aside.

Red Flag = White Flag

Being there for someone can cause you to be blind. You care for someone so much that you don't see what people see. That's okay, but always evaluate your situation from other people's perspectives. You can say "I don't care what people think" but that's not the point. The point is that if someone isn't appreciative of you or your time you should throw your red flag.

Throw your white flag at the first sight of a red flag.

To *Her*

I've been in this for a couple of months now.
We've been dealing for some time now.
I asked a bunch of questions and always got a no
so, I truly believed nothing was wrong.

He held me down in ways you couldn't imagine.
He was my right hand
when mines were lacking.
I was down to ride
like Aladdin.

Momma always told me
whatever happens in the dark
comes to light.
And that's what happened with you.
Baby Girl, I didn't know about you.
And when I found out about you
shit, it hurt me too.

Cause I was holding shit down
I was lending a helping hand.
I was feeding this man.
His mind, body and soul.
I'm talking about his pockets.

I'm talking multiple Benjamin
not just a couple of dollars.

It's clear now that I played the fool.
I don't have any words to explain.
I thought the best of him.
Just like a flower
I thought we had room to grow.
My mind was a little clouded
and I was going through a lot.
I really cared for this man
and well he cared for me not.

I truly want to apologize.
I know I was acting kind of blind.
Even after I found out about you
I continued so I truly apologize.
This is just an open letter
from the girl on the side.

I don't think I've ever fallen out of love with someone I've loved. I really don't think you ever fall out of love. Because if the love is real, it doesn't fade. If I've ever muttered the words "I love you" know that I still do. Because love doesn't fade. My love doesn't fade.

Love is unconditional and timeless.

A Fat Kid Loves Cake... Well I Love You.

I haven't washed the clothes
that I left behind
because they smell just like you.
Cherry Blossoms.
Funny thing is I don't like cherries
but all the time spent in your car
it never bothered me.

I guess it had something to do with the fact that
I was so lost in your eyes
that I was a little too emotionally high
to use any other senses.
Or maybe I was too focused on your touch
how you roughly gripped me up
but gentle touched my heart.
Too focused to use my fucking brain
and open up my mind
to what was really happening inside.

This was so convenient for you
you got your cake and you were eating it too.
It was like
me I loved you like a fat kid loves cake
but you loved to eat all the cake.

And me I was willing to share

because although my mind said no

my heart said go.

Because I didn't think you was gonna leave me alone.

You see I'm constantly so messed up

and my heads so screwed up

that even after knowing you'll choose her

I still had hope that eventually you would choose me.

You see I gave you my cake.

I mean literally you had whatever ass I have

and then some too.

You were like a spoiled kid I never said no to.

Gave you the milk whenever you want.

And I mean this in the most literal way possible.

You had all of me.

I mean had you been a little more secretive

with your ex bitch

Next bitch?

Whoever shit might've been.

You probably would've been able to slice this cake

and fill it with frosting.

Expectations With No Intentions

Relationships with no interest in being anything more.
Why be my significant other if that's all you saw?
Why couldn't you just stay my friend
avoid all the unnecessary what ifs.

Stop trying to be my lover
just for the benefits.
This is the most selfish
a man can get.

Don't string me along
if you don't mean any harm.
Cause eventually I'll want more.
I'll want a future
like the ones from the songs.
I'll wanna love you
the way you never did before.

Then you'll break my heart
how selfish of you.
Because after this
I won't know how to love anymore.
Because of you
it'll seem like hurt is all I know anymore.

Because I'll take you back
when you say you're sorry.
We'll repeat the cycle
until I break the cycle
leaving you "sorry".
I won't come back
there won't be anymore.
Don't try to be in a relationship
if you have no intention of being anything more.

Letter to the boys I've "loved"

Dear First Love,
You taught me well.
I never knew how to love much
or be affectionate at all.
Coming from a home where love was said
but never really shown.
You taught me how to love
someone besides myself.
Eventually, I forgot how to love me.
Not to blame you
but I was brainwashed.
This is when I lost me.

Dear Experimental Love,
Man, you made me feel different.
Took you awhile to get me
and the moment you got me shit flipped.
You taught me one thing
guys gossip more than girls.
Sad but true.
I can't wish you anything but the best.
We'll cross paths again.
I promise you.

Dear Spontaneous Love,

Never thought I would be able to feel so alive again.

Never thought I could smile again.

Never thought I'd meet someone to get it.

Get me, get the pain, the anxiety.

But I also never thought you would cause it.

Cause so much pain as you did.

And still, I promised whenever you need someone

whenever you need something

you have a friend in me.

A promise I would never break.

Dear Forever Love,

My love

I cannot find the words to say thank you.

My angel

you taught me how to love me again.

How to put me first.

My knight and shining armor

you came into my life at the perfect time.

At a time when I forgot how to love me

when I didn't know what love means.

My darling

I pray it's never bad blood

I pray we never fall apart.

Without you

I probably would've never been here.

So thank you for literally saving my heart.

Sincerely, the girl that loves you.

The one you might never love back.

All in all, you've all taught me one thing.

Pain is inevitable

and love hurts.

The only way it won't

Is if I ALWAYS love me first.

"No More Boyfriends"

When I say no more boyfriends
I mean it.
I want no more empty promises
no more broken hearts.
I don't want anymore, meaningless nights.

When I say no more boyfriends
I mean no more tears.
No more 3 A.M. bathroom cries
wondering why I'm just not enough
why I'm not right.
No more, having him go out
making me wonder.
Is he being faithful?
Is he being loyal?

I'm not Anti men.
I'm anti boyfriend.
"Boyfriend" is starting to just be a term.
Just a word
some letters put together
that literally means shit.

Maybe I'm falling for the wrong men

But wait let me explain.
I'm anti boyfriends
because I deserve some bling
This finger deserves a ring.
This heart doesn't deserve pain.
This mind deserves peace.

Opposites Don't Attract.

The problem with love is
someone loves too much
the other, not enough.
Or someone loves too hard
someone not hard enough.

Man, I just want consistency.
I want you to love me today
and not wake up tomorrow feeling differently.
I want you to love me for me
flaws and all.
I want you to watch me sleep
because it's peaceful.
But wake me up
because you miss my complaining.

I want you to miss me
when we're busy
when we haven't seen each other
because our schedules aren't syncing.
Don't miss me when I'm gone
when I choose to walk away.
Miss me the minute you walk out the door
because you wanted to stay.

Man, I would want you to stay.

I know baby you gotta make money.

But I'll send you a little text 30 minutes later

to let you know I wish you would've never left

and you send me a message back.

I don't mean a text response.

I mean a message later by actually coming back.

I want to feel the equality

between our love.

I don't wanna feel like I'm suffocating you

with all these feelings.

Because I love too hard

and fall too easy.

I want you to wish me.

Wish for me.

Pray for me.

Pray for us and all we can be.

I want you to want me

not more than I want you

just enough for me to feel like

"This man really loves me too"

Peace... I'm Out

I can detect
the slightest change
in the way people act with me.
I can detect the slightest unusual
sentence
word
breath.

It's a gift and a curse.
It's like a six sense.
I can tell when you're going to leave
before your actual words.
I can sense you being distant
before you even start.
I can smell the burning flame
the one that will tear us apart.
I can detect the slightest change
I can feel it in my heart.

I may sound a little crazy
but hear me out.
I like to leave before I am left.
So, peace …
I'm out.

A woman's intuition

A woman's intuition never lies
as bazaar as the idea is
I promise if it didn't happen yet
within a short time span it will.

I knew I was crazy to think God sent me you.
But I thought
you would never do me like that.
You are the devil in disguise.
But I thought
we just having fun.
There's nothing wrong dancing with the devil.
Until it became
premarital sex
and I'm yearning for your touch.
But I thought
god put you on my path for a reason.
He wouldn't do anything to be deceiving.

But after we've spent a short time
good sex, good vibes...
now I'm begging for a reply.
My gut is telling me you got what you wanted so you left.
You're being a little distant.

but my mind is telling me there's something missing
maybe I'm overthinking.
Maybe you are too busy to be persistent.

So
when Summer Walker drops her EP
I send out a text, "we need to talk"
because consistency is key.
"Is it bad?"
I don't know we'll see.
Because it all depends on what you tell me.
Because if my intuition is right
Like Faith Lee said "Karma is a bitch for you"
and I'm gonna be that bitch
coming around full circle
to fuck up yo' shit.
Because if you think you gon' play me
You got another think coming baby.

I knew I was crazy to think that God sent me you.
You are the devil in disguise
but nothing's wrong with dancing with the devil
as long as I remain wise
and remember
a woman's intuition never lies.

Reality...

I thought maybe this time would be different.
Maybe you'll come clean, apologize, becoming the person
I fell in love with.
But this isn't
High School Musical, Cinderella, Grey's
or any love story known.
This is reality.

And in reality
I feel like I made you pay.
I feel like I made you crawl, beg, plead on your knees.
Realizing that I wasn't quite in tune with reality.
Because it might've seemed like forever
a couple months or so in reality.
But in reality
I picked you up after two seconds and polished your
knees for you.
In reality, you now love me a little more
I love you a little less
ultimately, hating myself greater than before.

I thought maybe you've changed.

Seeing me grow and prosper made you regret causing so
much pain.
I thought maybe you'll take a step back
realizing all the ways I've loved you that someone else
couldn't.
Realizing I stayed, when someone else wouldn't.
You and I confused this for love.

When in reality
love isn't hurting someone.
Wait I'll give you this
maybe you do love me
maybe you do care
but someone who had the slightest respect for me
wouldn't even dare.
Because
I tried
I cried
and I pleaded
for you to
see me for me
love me for me
and want me for me.
So maybe I gotta go my own way.
Lose my glass slipper for someone else.

Because you aren't

The Troy to my Gabriella

The Prince to my Cinderella

The Shepard to my Meredith Grey

I'll soon become the one that just got away.

Her W's, Your L's

She sacrifices a lot for you.
You may not see it
but she loses a lot for you.
Not just sleep
but her sanity
her time
her friendships.
It all just goes for you.

Meanwhile
you sleep great at night.
And your boys they're always around.
She stops the world for you
calls out of work
just because she wants to spend some time with you.
Wait up till you're ready
because you said you'll stop by today.
Did it ever occur to you
she had a life before you?
Did it ever occur to you
that she's doing it all for you?

For you
the world stops

her world stops.
When you leave
her world won't start
until it crumples.
And you'll regret
the perfection you let go.

Because her wins
is your L's.
Her gains
is your fails.

Love vs. Lust

You got someone who loves you
why go entertain someone who lust you.
I need you to know the difference.

Ya may be going through things
it might be complicated now
but when you're down and out
when your pockets in a drought
the one who loves you
holds you down.
The one who lust you
is nowhere around.

You see
love is one complicated thing.
Sometimes you love too much
sometimes not enough.
Somethings you're trying to figure out
whether this is love or lust.

Don't go out there cheating.
Don't make her question her existence.
Love is more than a drug
it's a silent killer.

Love is allowing someone
to hold a gun to you heart
but trusting them not to pull the trigger.

All I want for Christmas is...

I had an urge today.
to grab my phone and text you.
Because I missed you.
Because the holidays aren't the same if I don't have you.

I had an urge today.
to pull up to your crib
with court side seats to your favorite NBA team.
Because you were the light of my life.
You were the reason I smiled.

I had an urge today.
To not fight back my mind
because my heart yearns for you.
And my body craves you.
Because these holidays aren't the same
if you aren't by my side.

I had an urge today.
To walk into your apartment
Singing "All I want is you"
because Christmas isn't Christmas without you.

I had an urge today.
And Snapchat doesn't make it any better.
All these memories of what could've been
what should've been.
But I am proud to say.

I had an urge today
and that's all it was.
As much as I'm yearning for your love
I'm also yearning for my own.

To my Father

You didn't come home last night
and it sort of validated everything I chose to ignore.
You didn't come home last night
and I swear that shit hurts deep in my core.
Because I defended you
more than I should have.
I defended you to people.
But most importantly
to my mind
to my heart
to my soul.

I didn't expect things to end like this
I didn't expect you to just walk away.
Ever since the news broke
I can't even look at you the same.
I tried my hardest to explain to myself
that this is just how life goes.
I tried so hard to refrain myself
from thinking you don't love your little girls.

But I can't.
I can't help but think
you chose another above we.

I can't help but think
you let someone take you away from this family.

Did you at least think of us?
Is there some good that comes out of this?
Maybe we'll get
two birthdays'
two Christmas'
but I can't have two weddings.

I just don't understand
just please give me some clarity.
I swear no one can break my heart
more than what my father did.

6 A.M

Reyna Biddy said,
"I wish my father wouldn't have cheated on my mother
and I wish it were easier to find a lover nothing like him"
and man did that hit me hard.
Because I wish that too.
Most importantly
I wish I didn't believe that was love.

Emotional abuse is one of the hardest things to endure.
Because you never know when it's happening
until after...
it's 3 a.m.
and you're in the bathroom crying
wondering why you aren't good enough.
Then it's 4 a.m.
and you're coming up with a plan
because you don't wanna hit depression again.
5 a.m.
You cry out to God
asking him why he doesn't take you
why doesn't he call you home?

6 a.m.
Your phone rings

and it's time to start your day.
And you know that by 7 a.m.
if no one gets a message from you
they will begin to worry
they'll know somethings up.
Some might even do pop ups.
So, you get up.
You have to go on about your day.
You paint that smile on your face
and go on your way.

Well I'm here to tell you
it's okay to not be okay.
But at 3 a.m.
tell yourself you're good enough
you are beautiful
you are smart.
At 4 a.m.
tell yourself it's okay not to be okay
there's no plan to be made
because you're gonna live another day.
Because at 5 a.m.
God isn't gonna take you
because you serve a bigger purpose
and baby girl you are worth it.

So, at 6 a.m.

dry your eyes

and go on about your life.

Because you are perfect

you serve a purpose

and you are worth it.

"Glass Slipper"

I'm trying to shatter the glass ceiling.
I'm trying to do what others doubt I can
because I am Black
because I am Hispanic
because I am a woman.
I don't wanna step into the glass slipper.
I wanna slip my way right on into something
"I can't have"

"You shouldn't be here"
Well, I'm here to stay.
This isn't a man's world
this is a world for all.
I don't wanna step into the glass slipper
I wanna climb to the top
shatter that glass ceiling.
To then realize
there's another one there.
Another one that I'm going to shatter soon.

There's no feeling that I can't
because I know I can.
There's no feeling of doubt
because I know I will.

Why would I step into the glass slipper?
When I can break the glass ceiling?
Glass was made to be broken
and this glass ceiling I will break.

Your Fatal Flaw

Sometimes your best quality
can be your fatal flaw.
Your best quality
can be the greatest cause
to all your pain and suffering.

You care
way too much for people
way to fast
when you don't receive it back.

You love way too hard
way too large.
Sometimes you have to love with guard.

Love from a distant
because love is many people's weaknesses.
Care from a far
bear arms anytime someone gets near.

Close your heart a little
and open their minds.
Don't give so much
give a piece

to keep your peace
treasure your sanity.

It's okay to love.
It's okay to care.
Just remember to
love yourself
care for you
and do for you.

Don't lose yourself being you.
Don't allow your best quality
to be your greatest pain.
Use your brain
to assist your heart.
Don't allow you best quality
to be the main reason you fall apart.

Self-Reflect --

Love that is unconditional, pure and genuine is super hard to find. Especially in this generation where love is something people aren't seeking. But having that quality is a blessing and a curse. If you are able to love someone hard, unconditionally, and it's genuine with no interest you are rare.

You are a rare gem that nobody knows how to deal with. Your walls might become so high because you've been loved so dry. I can't express this enough, do not let the pain change this quality. Understand that not everybody is not deserving of this quality. Although this might seem like your worst quality to you, it's your best. Just don't allow people to take advantage. Learn to stay ten toes to your love, but also yourself.

The Odds Against Me

They tried to break me
but I prevailed.
Black women in America
they thought I was destined to fail.

Look at me here
on the verge of a degree.
Nothing wrong with early pregnancies
but here I am
20 with no babies.

Told momma they tried to knock me down
promised her I will not fail.
Gotta look at her in the eyes when I hit that stage.
I promised her a D.
Well that promise is broken
because I'm bringing back three.
Not just a diploma
but two degrees.

The odds were never in my favor
but I'll beat the odds in many flavors.
I don't wanna sound typical
but they betted against me.

I guess they were ready to lose.

Because I will prevail.

I'm destined for greatness.

You'll eventually see

the only person that can successfully work against me

is me.

What is Growth?

Growth is constantly confused for a lot of things.
But what is it really?
Growth isn't not loving someone who's toxic.
If you fall you fall
but growth is being able to love them from afar
because you realize you guys aren't good for each other.

Growth is co-existing, co-parenting.
Because if you can be grown enough to make a baby
you can be grown enough to raise a baby
despite your feelings for the other parent.

Growth is understanding that people change
and sometimes it doesn't have to do anything with you.
Growth is understanding how to maintain a relationship
through disagreements.
Because not everybody has the same mindset as you
not everybody believes the same things you do.
Being able to interact with different people is growth.

Growth is losing the argument
because it shouldn't matter who said what last
because you're afraid of losing that person.
Growth is being able to let go.

Not every issue needs a conversation
sometimes just an internal realization.
Growth is meeting someone halfway.
Growth is realizing that sometimes you aren't right
and if you can't accept that, you aren't growing.
Growth is learning to love peace.

Dear College Girl,

You are now entering a different atmosphere
because it might've been a "Hot Girl Summer"
but we need to get into this "Nerd Girl Fall".
And whether it's year one, year three or even year four
there is a fight to be won.
Against a system that might seem like it's designed for
failure.
Because you're 4.0 seems far during midterm
but during finals you can hit that home run.
You can turn it around, just like your behavior.

It may be hard
adjusting to work, school and a social life
some even a sport.
I'm not going to tell you it won't be tiring because it will.
And us as women alone go through enough
mentally, emotionally and physically.
Just being a woman is hard enough.
But that's what makes this easier.
You are designed for toughness.
You are designed to have a lot on your plate and eat it up.

And to the girl who is heartbroken on top of this.
Use it as motivation

one up your broken heart regardless of the reason.
Because Momma's sick, and Daddy's not around
or the guy you loved dipped in the beginning of the
summer season.
You level up and deal.
You adjust and kill.

And when you're struggling with midterms and finals
always remember this
have your mental break down
then go fight it through.
We may live in a system of injustice
but you are designed for toughness
and everything around you may seem to fail
but you
you will prevail.

Dear Momma,

It's hard to put into words the love I have for you.
It's hard to say thank you because where do I start?
But thank you for being who you are.
Thank you for not covering the sky
because now I know
life isn't easy.
Nothing is going to get handed to me.

I just hope one day I can live up to become
half the Daughter you are
half the Sister you are
half the Mother you are
half the Wife you were.
I hope one day I will be
half of the women you are!
Period.

But thanks again.
You've love me unconditionally
but never let me off easy.
And because of that I now know
I can hold things down all on my own.

Momma's Words

My mom always told me "if he really likes you, he'll be your friend until you can date". In my natural me fashion I didn't listen, but that's my favorite piece of advice. Many men think just because you don't commit you don't like them. I've loved a man to death and couldn't commit in fear of ruining the friendship. I couldn't commit because I wasn't emotionally ready. So, I said, "If you really like me and want to be with me, you'll wait until I'm ready." Just because you aren't ready to commit doesn't mean you don't like or love someone. Not being ready to enter a relationship doesn't mean anything about the relationship itself, it means you need some self-care. Being able to build yourself to the person you want to be. Personal growth.

Yours demons can ruin anything if they aren't addressed privately.

To my sisters

For you
the world stops.
And I don't mean pause
because you don't wanna miss your favorite part.
I mean STOP
Like I'll drop whatever I'm doing to rush by your side.
I mean if I need to take some time
away from me for you
I'll do that, I got you.
If I need to struggle to just see ya shine
I promise that's what I will do.

To my sisters
for you my life has changed
for you I WILL NOT play.
Nobody could fight with you but me.
I'll put my life on the line you'll see.
I don't care what we're up against
I don't care who's by your side
I promise that as long as you have me
you'll ALWAYS be alright.

To my sisters
I don't say this a lot

but I love you with everything in me.

Everything I do is for you.

Just wait and you'll see.

To the first girl I've Love

You came into my life when I needed you to.
I was coming out of a dark place
you became the light at the end of the tunnel
the one who keeps me awake.

I don't know when it happened
all I know is that it did.
We're falling for each other
like some silly little kids.

Your smile
it's amazing.
Every day you amaze me.
And your accent
drives me crazy.
But my mind can get used to this
and my heart will fall.

I've got sleepless nights
and I'm tired in the morning.
But all of that's okay
I guess I'm high off your love.

To the first girl I love

you're pretty amazing.
My heart is blazing
waiting for your love.

To the first girl I've ever loved (After Love)

No offense, but out of every girl I've encountered
for you to make me fall in love is bazaar.
I didn't expect to fall
and I didn't expect you to break my heart.
And even after everything
my love still hasn't stopped.

This was something new to me
not so new to you.
Part of me feels like you used me.
Part of me feels like this wasn't real.

I kind of feel like this was all lies
all for your own comfort.
You love a guy
and I was just a number.

But for me this was real
I don't play with feelings
I always keep it thorough.
Honesty's the best policy
then why did you lie to me.

As much as we were different

we were one in the same.

we shared similar pains

and had similar hurt.

The red flags threw up an alert

but still I didn't listen.

To the fact that you had shitty ass communication skills

until you became distant.

And the physical distance couldn't keep us apart

but yet you still decided to tore up my heart.

As much as it hurt me

I know I'll be okay.

I'll just be another one.

One that got away.

Abandoned Myself

I keep trying to figure out
where my abandonment issues came from.
I keep blaming
my dad leaving
and my exes never stick around.
But I haven't taken the chance to
look at the person in the mirror.

The more these issues arise
the more my heart breaks
from someone walking out my life
I'm beginning to realize
it's no one's blame but my own.
Because I constantly see myself allowing people to walk
all over me.
Because I'm "too nice"
because "I like you"
because I'm "too weak".
Honestly
I'm just too emotional.
Because when I like, I like deep.
Because when I love it's to get married.

I'm disappointing myself

by staying and waiting

thinking that one day you'll change ways.

I keep saying "I know my love run deep"

and you'll look for me.

But still I stay.

Because I don't ever wanna leave like I have been left.

I don't wanna hurt someone how I've been hurt.

So, I wait till you leave.

I wait until you abandon me

ultimately abandoning myself.

Solid to me

As solid as you are to someone, your actions can be solid to them, but it can be abandoning yourself. Always self-reflect, think how do things hinder me? Do I benefit? Not to say everything has to be beneficial, but I always tend to help and benefit others and remain stuck. You have goals, dreams and standards. Don't neglect yourself because you wanna remain solid and "ten toes down".

Self-neglect is worse than any neglect you'll ever experience.

Love, You don't.

You don't break a heart.
You don't hurt someone whose only intention was to
love you.
You don't leave unexpectedly.
Even if she isn't your girlfriend
you give her the decency of honesty.
You don't lead her on
and if you do it unintentionally
you immediately realize and pull away.
Give her the respect she deserves.
And never make her feel less than.
You be gentle
and kind.

You be there for her
in her darkest moments.
Even if things are a little ugly
you hold her and make sure she's perfectly fine.
Because she would do the same for you.

You console her.
You comfort her.
You do not rescue her to then be the cause of her pain.
Because that is the biggest "fuck boy" shit ever known.

Do not kiss and tell.
Okay, maybe that's the biggest "fuck boy" shit ever.

You treasure her
every moment
every second.
You don't compel her to believe that this is something
that it's not.
As much as your head below your waist wants you to
you don't use her for sex.

Do not make her compete
for your time
your heart
your attention.
You make her know she's number one.

You don't find her
scoop her
make her believe you're different
make her believe in love again
just to show her
all the reasons she's doubted it in the first place.
You are to never make her tell you how to be a man
her man.
Because you are

to love her unconditionally
or leave her alone.

Do make her happy
never make her feel alone.

Together but Alone...

The worst thing in the world is being in a crowded room and feeling alone. Imagine being in a relationship and feeling single. You live together but you're going to sleep alone. You love them, but they constantly break your heart. When in a relationship you should never feel alone whether they are near or far. Being in a relationship has this fulfillment that nothing else can fulfill. The feeling of companionship shouldn't go away.

It's not love, it's wholeness.

Self-Protection: A Villanelle

You Love way to hard
Way too large
Sometimes you should love with guard.

Your heart maybe a little scarred.
Your ex deserves some kind of charge but you
You love way too hard.

He certainly had no regard
For you and your big heart. Which is why
Sometimes you should love with guard.

Soon your heart will be unscarred
Simply when you realize
You love way too hard.

Be your own safeguard
Shelter your own heart
Sometimes you should love with guard.

Keep your own scorecard
Close your little heart because
You love way too hard.
Sometimes you should love with guard.

Dear Twenty-One,

I want you to love,
like twenty didn't break you.
But guard your heart enough
to show how much twenty made you.
I want you to remove that fear of change
and step out of your comfort zone
because that's the way to ensure growth.

I want you to love you.
Although twenty loved you too
but unconditional.
I want you to love you first.
Because rule number one
is to never be number two.

Understand that timing is everything
and you cannot wait for others that do not wait for you.
Understand that time is going fast.
So, tell people that you love them.
But don't wait around to be abused and misused.

Understand that twenty is for growth.
So, although you may believe
that you should have it all together

where you are now is perfectly fine.
Your timing couldn't be better.

Myiaa's Outro:

I guess you can say you know my story now. Everything I've experienced, my innermost feelings, things I've never confessed to anyone. I never knew I wanted to be a writer, I thought maybe I'll be a psychologist or something. It wasn't until 8th grade, when I was in English class and had to write a poem. I lost it. But I remember everybody telling me it was so good. Then when I got to high school and we entered our poetry unit I knew this was something I could see myself doing. Now I'm here at 22, in my fourth college year, finishing my first summer semester, stressed but finally putting myself out there. Nervous and scared, but I have faith in my work. This is me spreading my truth. I have constantly been misunderstood, and never heard. This is my story.

To anyone who can relate, I hear you. I know what it feels like. I know how hard it is to navigate life with a broken heart. I know what it's like to feel abandoned and left more than you are loved and held. I know what it's like to let yourself go and lose your last brain cell because you are hurt. I know what it's like to hold your cry at night so that no one will hear. Or to be at a family gathering faking it.

I understand what it's like to live in a world of injustice. I understand what it's like to be scared. Scared for your parents, your siblings, your loved ones to walk outside. I understand what it's like to try to hold it altogether when the world around you is falling apart.

I know what it's like to question your ability. I know what it's like to doubt that you are a good sister, daughter, friend, girlfriend. I have been in those shoes. I have been in places where I didn't think I can ever get out. Funks so bad that I never thought I would get over. I am here as living proof that things do get better.

You will get better.

Keep up with me on my social media for first-hand information on the next projects, different content, Q&A's and many other exclusives.

Personal Instagram: @_Myia_x
Writers Instagram: @Myiaa.thewriter
Twitter: @Myiaa_thewriter

Made in the USA
Coppell, TX
03 December 2020

42929540R00069